MAGICAL SPOT WHAT

Nick Bryant & Rowan Summers

HINKLER BOOKS

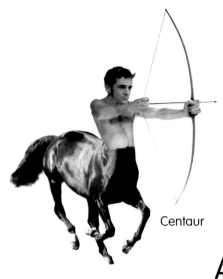

Centaur

Big Bad Wolf

Also Available In This Series

Spot What Picture Hunt
Spot What Amazing
Spot What Spectacular

First published in 2005 by Hinkler Books Pty. Ltd.
17 - 23 Redwood Drive, Dingley, Vic, 3172, Australia.

HB
HINKLER
BOOKS

Printed and bound in China.

Cockle Shell

Knight

Bassoon

Dragon

Emu

Bowler Hat

Contents

Knight

Egg

Dodo

Can you spot
A candlestick,
An alarm clock,
And a lion,
A frog, a snail,
A puppy dog's tail,
A soldier,
And an iron?

Can you find five
Rubber ducks,
Three mice and a
Gingerbread man,
Three silver bells,
Four cockle shells,
A moon and a
Watering can?

Can you spot a bowler hat,
An eggbeater, a toaster,
Two chickens and a cherry,
A piano, a roller coaster?

Can you find a bicycle,
A pencil and a flipper,
Two bubbles and a joker,
A windmill and a zipper?

Can you spot three radios,
A paint brush and a spring,
An icicle, five vehicles,
A kite, a reel of string?

Can you find a ping-pong ball,
Five flowers and a lock,
A ladybug, three butterflies,
A cactus and a clock?

Can you spot a candy cane,
A pair of pointy shoes,
A heart of gold, a peacock,
An egg and three emus?

Can you find the planet earth,
A clover and two fours,
A car, a boat, a train, a plane,
A sleigh and Santa Claus?

Program

Can you spot a cowboy,
A doctor and a nurse,
Six robots, two teapots,
A parrot and a purse?

Can you find a snowflake,
Someone fast asleep,
A hen, a fox, a jack-in-the-box,
And three of Bo Peeps' sheep?

THE LILLIPUT AMATE
MAGICAL MAX AND H

CAPTAIN CONTRAPTION AND HIS AMAZING INVENTIONS

SS MAGICAL

BANG

Can you spot Napoleon,
A lollipop, a flute,
A camera and a daisy,
A yo-yo and squashed fruit?

Can you find a saxophone,
A telephone, two crowns,
A tambourine, a flying machine,
A watch, a wand, three clowns?

FOR ONE NIGHT ONLY

Can you spot a rhinocerous,
A sheep dog and a shepherd,
A big bad wolf, three little pigs,
A spinning wheel, a leopard?

Can you find three elephants,
A camel and a llama,
A dodo, a stork, an old pitchfork,
Three goats, and an iguana?

Can you spot an onion,
A horseshoe and a spoon,
A quill and four chess pieces,
A harp and a bassoon?

Can you find three sea shells,
A dogfish and a brain,
A fan, a mortar and pestle,
A lamp, a candle flame?

The Almanac of Handy Hexe

Can you spot a centaur,
Three skulls, a golden horn,
A scorpion, two griffins,
A witch, a leprechaun?

Find the Loch Ness Monster,
Three unicorns, a key,
A telescope, the pipes of Pan,
A fish, a dove and a bee?

fountain of youth

Hoodwink & Mesmer

EMPORIUM of PRESTIDIGITATION

Hoodwink & Mesmer

SHOPLIFTERS will be turned into TOADS

WITCHES WEEKLY

WISHING UPON A STAR

How to Hex friends and influence people

NEW SUPERSTITIONIST
Can there be Golden Eggs without the guilt?

13 unlucky things to do.

Ask about Vexes Curs

FORTUNE Teller 500
Tea Leaves: telling it like it IS!

NEXT YEAR: A REVIEW

Better Gnomes and Covens.

Slugs & snails & Puppy dogs tale

to avoid Evil Eye

Pixie Brand Magic Du

SPOT WHAT

22

Can you spot a gargoyle,
Three mirrors and a moose,
A gnome, a coin, a violin,
A shuttlecock, a goose?

Can you find an hourglass ,
Two swords and a troll,
A pixie and a pyramid,
A boat and a voodoo doll?

SULTAN
magic carpets

NEW
SEASON
BROOMS

COMPLETE RANGE OF
TALISMANS

NEW STOCKS
Scrolls &
Parchment

MAGIC
BEENZ

FOR
SALE

POTIONS
Freshly
Brewed

NEW & USED
SPELL
BOOKS
FOR SALE

WANDS
ALL SHAPES
AND SIZES

TROLL
STRENGTH
POTION

FAIRY
CURSE REMOVER
GODMOTHER

100% PURE
Hobgoblin
ELBOW GREASE

OCTOBER
31
HALLOWEEN

OCTOBER
30
Saturday

OCTOBER
29
Friday

OCTOBER
28
Thursday

Can you spot a wagon wheel,
A rooster and a crow,
A pirate and three apples,
Two ghosts and a wheelbarrow?

Can you find the invisible man,
Two sacks, an axe, a skunk,
A hearse, a horse, a haunted house,
Three witches hats and a trunk?

SHEE'S
APPLES

FUNERALS 'R' US

FOR
SALE

RIP
BUBBLES THE
GOLDFISH
1999 - 2000
SADLY WE SAY
GOODBYE TO
OUR DEAR FISH

Can you spot two reindeer,
Two penguins and a bear,
A letterbox, three pine cones,
A fireplace and a chair?

Can you find a snowman,
A puppy and four cars,
A sailboat and a dinosaur,
Two tops and two guitars?

MAGICAL

See if you can spot these things in every picture:

Can you find the words 'SPOT WHAT',
A crystal ball, a cat,
A knight, a dragon, a wizard,
An owl and a black top hat?

Obelisk

Pine Cone

Flying Machine

Rules For The Spot What Game

1. Flip a coin to see who goes first.

2. The winner of the coin toss chooses an item from the book for the other person to find, saying, for example, 'Can you spot a candlestick?'.

3. The spotter must then find the item.

4. If the spotter can't find the item the winner shows them where it is and gets another turn.

6. If the spotter can find the item, then he or she gets 5 points and it's his or her turn.

7. The first to reach 30 points wins but you could also set your own limit of 50, or even 100 points or...

...simply play best out of three.

Happy Spotting!

You can also make the game more interesting by putting a time limit of one to three minutes on the search. Try making up your own games too!

Peacock

Gargoyle

The Spot What Challenge

The following items are much harder to find so get ready for the challenge.

Leprechaun

Moose

Imagine
(page 4/5)

A heart
6 paper planes
An apple
A golden egg
An abacus
FI 130
A family

Rainbow
(page 8/9)

A bee
5 telephones
2 snakes
A pair of gloves
2 drums
A funnel
2 pairs of scissors

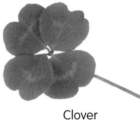

Clover

Magic
(page 6/7)

A domino
A boomerang
A canoe
A nut and bolt
A lightbulb
A key
An eye spying

Wish
(page 10/11)

A winning hand
A bride and groom
7 pots of gold
A pineapple
An arched window
2 Christmas trees
3 lemons

Napoleon

Griffin

Radio

Sled

Audience
(page 12/13)

A snake
Sunglasses
A soccer ball
A volley ball
A football
A tennis ball
Knitting

Castle
(page 16/17)

Rapunzel
3 kings
A rooster
A mousetrap
Quasimodo
A pocket watch
A pirate flag

Mortar
and Pestle

Stage
(page 14/15)

A set of keys
A puffin
A vase
A penny farthing
A torch
A pen
A banana peel

Laboratory
(Page 18/19)

A centaur
The solar system
A chocolate frog
A goose
2 butterflies,
A coffee mug
An umbrella

Spinning Wheel

Windmill

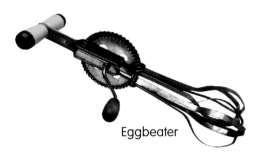

Eggbeater

Pointy Shoes

Myths

(page 20/21)

The sun
The tooth fairy
Excalibur
The magic harp
A woodpecker
An obelisk
A tallship

Halloween

(page 24/25)

Headless horseman
2 candelabras
An oilcan
A cowardly lion
3 lanterns
2 pumpkin pies
9 skulls

Snowflake

Emporium

(page 22/23)

A saw
A hammer
A pair of pliers
A clamp
2 axes
A dart
3 wands

Christmas

(page 26/27)

2 gingerbread men
3 snowflakes
5 sleds
A pogo stick
A woolly mitten
A birdhouse
Spectacles

Telephone

Quasimodo

Excalibur

Witch's Hat

Pan

Acknowlegements

Special thanks to the following people:

Toby Bishop
Kendra Bishop
Kate Bryant
Samantha Boardman
Christopher Timms
Sam Bryant
Derek Debenham
Rod and Mary Bryant
Sante Cigany
Sam Grimmer
Peter Tovey Studios
Louise Coulthard
Silvana Paolini
Paul Scott
Tracey Ahern
Stephen Ungar
Stephen Bishop
Ruth Coleman
Everyone at Hinkler Books

**CGI Backgrounds for Castle, Stage, Audience
and Emporium by Steve Evans
s_evans42@yahoo.com**

Penny Farthing

Dogfish

Voodoo Doll